In Touch With Nature
Living
Things

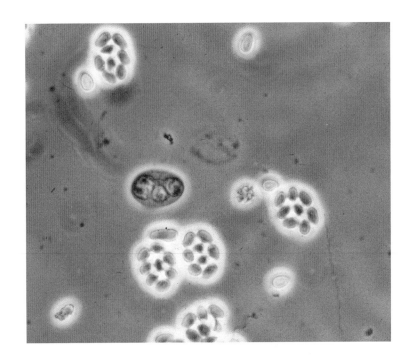

BLACKBIRCH®
PRESS

THOMSON
GALE

San Diego • Detroit • New York • San Francisco • Cleveland • New Haven, Conn. • Waterville, Maine • London • Munich

PHOTOGRAPHIC CREDITS
Art Explosion: 29l; **Image Ideas Inc:** 26t, 29br, 30tl, 30bl, 30tr, 30brl; **Newscast:** AstraZeneca 3, 23; **NOAA:** OAR/NURP 6–7; **Photodisc:** 4–5, 14–15, 18–19, 22–23, 24–25, 28; **PHIL:** 9t, 10–11; **Science Photo Library:** Chris Bjornberg 5t; **USDA/ARS:** Peggy Greb 29tr, David Williams 1.

Step-by-step photography throughout: Martin Norris

Front cover: Martin Norris and Photodisc

Consultant: Mark Hostetler, Ph.D.,
 Assistant Professor, Extension Wildlife Specialist,
 Department of Wildlife Ecology & Conservation,
 IFAS, University of Florida

For The Brown Reference Group plc
Editorial and Design: John Farndon and Angela Koo
Picture Researcher: Helen Simm
Illustrations: Darren Awuah
Managing Editor: Bridget Giles
Art Director: Dave Goodman
Children's Publisher: Anne O'Daly
Production Director: Alastair Gourlay
Editorial Director: Lindsey Lowe

LIBRARY OF CONGRESS CATALOGING-IN-PUBLICATION DATA

Available from the Library of Congress.

ISBN: 1-4103-0122-2

Contents

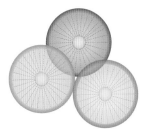

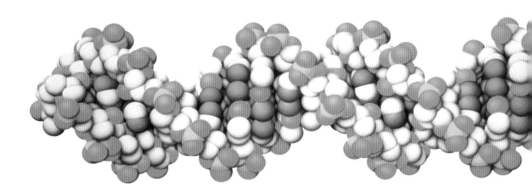

What is life?

Did you know?
The world's tiniest forms of life are bacteria called mycoplasmas. They are 1/250,000 inch (a millionth of a millimeter) long.

The Earth abounds with life. The land is covered with plants and animals. The oceans and the sky are filled with life. Indeed, there are living things in every tiny nook and cranny of Earth, and every environment no matter how extreme. There is life everywhere from the bitterly cold ice of the Antarctic to scorching volcanic hot springs.

Altogether, there are 10 million or more different kinds, or species, of living things. They range in size from microscopic bacteria to gigantic blue whales. They come in an astonishing variety of shapes and sizes.

It is easy to recognize a living thing. Everyone can tell that a butterfly or cow is alive, while a brick or a car is not. It is usually easy to tell when something is dead, too. Yet it is much harder to define just what exactly life is.

To try to narrow down just what is meant by life, some scientists say that all living things share certain characteristics (see Close-up: Five signs of life). Not every organism (a single living thing) has all of them. One characteristic is movement, and some plants move only as they grow. Even nonliving things may have some of these life characteristics. Crystals grow, for instance, and robots move and respond. All the same, together these features give a good picture of what living things have in common.

Living world
There is a huge range of life even in a small area like this, from the moose to microscopic bacteria.

CLOSE-UP *Five signs of life*

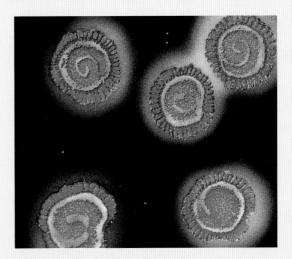

Viruses are much, much smaller than bacteria, and have no living cell. They can only multiply by taking over host cells. So scientists disagree over whether they are alive.

Anything that shows most or all of the following signs is likely to be a living thing.

Reproduction: All living things can make others like themselves.
Growth: Many organisms can grow steadily bigger, up to a certain size.
Metabolism: All living things can convert chemicals to get energy.
Movement: Most living things move in some way, even if the movement is small, like a plant's leaves turning toward the sun.
Response: Most living things react in some way to changes in their surroundings.

Did you know?
The world's tiniest viruses are parvoviruses. They are one 25 millionth inch (0.000000001 meters) long.

How life began

Did you know?
Ancient stromatolites grew in very tall cones up to 300 feet (100 m) high.

No one knows quite how life on Earth began. Most religions have their own creation story that tells the origins of life. Scientists have various theories, but it all happened so long ago that it is hard to be certain.

Scientists have found patterns in ancient rocks in western Australia. Many believe these patterns were left by microscopic living things called cyanobacteria (see page 31) more than 3.5 billion years ago. If so, they were among the first living things on Earth, though not actually the first. Earth itself is more than 4.6 billion years old.

The very beginning

When it first formed, Earth was a seething mass of volcanoes and smoke, constantly struck by rocks from space. Life could only begin once Earth cooled down a little and the rain of rocks ceased. That took 600 million years. So life could not have begun more than 3.9 billion years ago.

Scientists agree that life began with substances called organic chemicals. They are called organic chemicals because they are chemicals from which all living things or organisms are made. Organic chemicals occur naturally throughout the universe. By themselves, they are lifeless. But scientists believe that long ago some joined by chance in such a way that they could not only grow,

CLOSE-UP *Stromatolites*

The oldest signs of life on Earth are stony mounds called stromatolites. Some are billions of years old. Although long since turned to stone, they were formed by living things. They were slimy mats made by huge colonies of bacteria, with a thin layer of cyanobacteria on top. Cyanobacteria grow by soaking up the sun's energy, just like plants. The bacteria fed off dead cyanobacteria.

ON THE TRACK *Pond life*

Life may have begun in water. Most ponds are full of microscopic life. If you can use a microscope, you may be able to see some of these in a sample of pond water. All are made from a single cell.

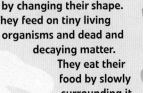

2. Diatoms are tiny algae (see page 30) with hard shells. They float near the water's surface. As plants do, they absorb sunlight to get the energy to make their own food.

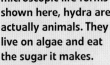

4

5

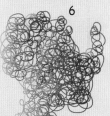

4. *Gleocapsa* are cyanobacteria (see Close-up: Stromatolites) that form a dark slime on rocks.

5. Unlike the other microscopic life forms shown here, hydra are actually animals. They live on algae and eat the sugar it makes.

1. Amoeba are microscopic life forms that move by changing their shape. They feed on tiny living organisms and dead and decaying matter. They eat their food by slowly surrounding it.

3. Spirogyra are a kind of algae. Individual organisms are tiny. But they form into long green strands that float in dense mats in rivers. The strands are sometimes called mermaid's tresses.

6. Like cyanobacteria, rhodospirillum is a bacteria that makes its own food using sunlight. While cyanobacteria make oxygen, these microscopic life forms do not.

6

1

3

but also reproduce. Life probably began when, again by chance, some of these amazing chemicals formed themselves into tiny packets. These tiny packets of chemicals then formed the very first living cells (see Living cells, pages 10–11), which are called archaebacteria.

On Earth or in space?

All life on Earth is descended from these archaebacteria. A few scientists think archaebacteria rained down on Earth to begin life, like seeds landing in soil. Most scientists, though, think it all started right here on Earth. Today archaebacteria still live in hot volcanic muds and hot springs.

Did you know?
Not all life began in water. Tiny bacteria could have begun life far underground inside rocks.

Microlife

The most plentiful forms of life are so tiny they can be seen only with a microscope. Most of these microscopic life forms, or microorganisms, are made from a single packet or cell (see Living cells, pages 10–11). There are many different kinds, from viruses only visible under powerful electron microscopes to giant jellylike amoebas. The most common by far are bacteria. But all are found in huge numbers almost everywhere on Earth. They float in air and water, coat rocks, and live on skin, inside bodies, and in soil. Even puddles that look lifeless are probably teeming with microlife. Bacteria, algae, fungi, and even tiny insects can quickly take over a pond, as this experiment shows.

A single spoonful of pond water can contain thousands of tiny protozoa like this amoeba. Protozoa are tiny, shapeless, and made from just one cell. But, like animals, they eat food. They surround it with their baglike bodies.

Did you know?

A dark, jellylike mass that creeps over damp wood is called slime mold. It is a mass of countless amoebas.

MAKE YOUR OWN LIVING PUDDLE

You will need:

✔ A handful of soil
✔ Partly decayed leaves
✔ Fresh leaves
✔ Dead grass
✔ A clear jar
✔ A magnifying glass
✔ A measuring cup

1 Make your own artificial puddle for the experiment by filling a clear jar with cold water from the faucet. Pour the water in until the jar is about two-thirds full.

2 Tear up the leaves and grass and push them down into the water. Drop in a handful of soil. Carefully shake or stir the jar to mix up the contents. Leave the jar to stand by a sunny window.

CLOSE-UP *Bacteria*

Bacteria are so tiny a hundred would fit on the period at the end of this sentence. Each is a single cell: a bag filled with a gel-like fluid and small objects called organelles. Some bacteria are autotrophic. That means they make food for themselves from chemicals, or from sunlight as plants do. Most are heterotrophic. That means they feed off other organisms. Many feed on dead organisms. These bacteria play a vital role in breaking down organic matter and recycling the chemicals it contains. Other heterotrophic bacteria find a living host. Some of these bacteria live on and inside the bodies of animals, including humans. Some bacteria help their host. Bacteria that live in the human intestine help digestion. They even help produce vitamins the body needs. Some bacteria cause diseases, such as pneumonia, and are called germs.

Puddle life

After three weeks, your puddle will look different. The water will be teeming with microorganisms. Of course, most are too small to see even with a magnifying glass. But you can identify some by their effect on the water (see list at right). What grows depends on the size of the jar, sunlight, the temperature, and the food. There can be up to 80 kinds of life forms. They belong to one of four major groups: bacteria, protists, algae, and fungi (see page 30).

What you see	What is growing
✸ Gold or brown mat at the bottom	Diatoms
✸ Slimy patches at the bottom	Protozoa
✸ Green water	Green algae
✸ Thin green threads	Green algae
✸ Dark bluish green coated mat	Cyanobacteria
✸ Pinkish water	Whiplike algae

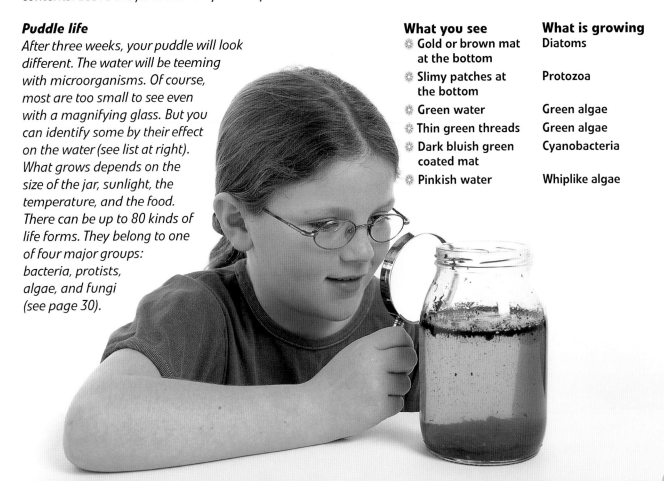

Living cells

Nearly all living things are built from tiny parcels called cells. The cells are so small they can only be seen under a microscope. Each cell is a living, dynamic chemical factory. Each has its own role to play in the life of the plant or animal of which it is part.

A living cell is basically a baglike case held together by a thin skin or membrane. This membrane has tiny holes that let certain chemicals in to feed the cell and let waste chemicals out.

Inside the membrane is a gel-like mixture. This provides a store of chemicals for the cell to use to build materials the body or plant needs. In the mixture are small objects called organelles. Different cells have different organelles, each with its own task. Many cells, for example, have sausage-shaped structures called mitochondria. Mitochondria are the cell's power plants. They convert the chemical energy in food into a form the cell can use to grow, divide, and do its work. The endoplasmic reticulum makes and stores vital substances. Together the mixture and organelles make up the cytoplasm.

CLOSE-UP *Animal cells*

Animals are made up of countless tiny cells. Each animal cell is a tiny bag filled with a gel-like substance dotted with organelles. The bag is a soft and flexible membrane. Unlike a plant cell, an animal cell has no tough cell wall, so it does not have a rigid shape. Inside the bag is a nucleus, which controls the cell. Outside the nucleus are the various organelles. Animal cells cannot make their own food. To survive, they must take it in from outside.

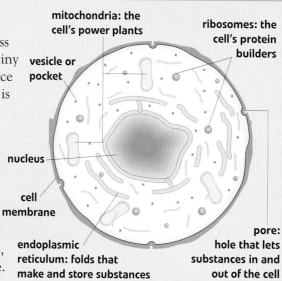

mitochondria: the cell's power plants

ribosomes: the cell's protein builders

vesicle or pocket

nucleus

cell membrane

endoplasmic reticulum: folds that make and store substances

pore: hole that lets substances in and out of the cell

CLOSE-UP *Plant cells*

Like animals, plants are made up of a huge number of tiny cells. But plant cells are very different from animal cells. Like animal cells, they are surrounded by a cell membrane. Yet in plants, the membrane is encased by a tougher wall of cellulose. This wall is light and strong and gives the cell its shape. Neighboring cell walls are fastened together with cellulose, too, so the plant can hold itself upright. Inside plant cells are some of the same organelles that animal cells have, but most plant cells also contain chloroplasts and vacuoles. Chloroplasts are organelles that only plant cells have. They are bright green and allow the plant to make its own food from water and air using the sun's energy. Vacuoles are storage cavities filled with a watery fluid called cell sap.

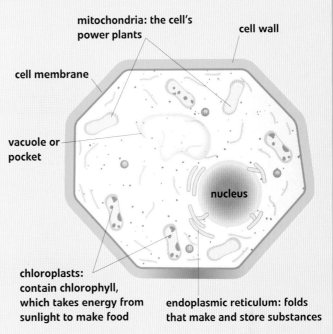

mitochondria: the cell's power plants

cell wall

cell membrane

vacuole or pocket

nucleus

chloroplasts: contain chlorophyll, which takes energy from sunlight to make food

endoplasmic reticulum: folds that make and store substances

Red blood cells
Human blood contains billions of tiny red blood cells. 40,000 blood cells would fit inside this O.

Curled up somewhere inside every living cell is also a long threadlike chemical called DNA. DNA is the cell's controller. It holds the cell's instructions for life in coded form. It tells the cell how to perform all its tasks and provides all the instructions to make an exact copy of the entire plant or animal.

In plant and animal cells, the DNA is held inside a little parcel in the center of the cell called the nucleus. Cells that have a nucleus are called eukaryotes. Bacteria and many other microorganisms have no nucleus, and are called prokaryotes.

Did you know?
The human body is made up of 10 trillion (10,000,000,000,000) tiny cells of many kinds.

Chemical factories

Living cells are tiny factories that constantly take in the chemicals they need, process them, and expel waste. The membrane, or outer skin of every cell, has tiny pores that let the chemicals ooze in and out in two main ways.

One way is by "active transport," in which chemicals called proteins pump in the things the cell needs and remove waste.

Another way is by osmosis (see Close-up: Osmosis). This is the way a cell pumps water in from outside. This vital process helps cells keep the mix of water and chemicals inside in just the right balance all the time—no matter what the mix of chemicals outside is. The experiment here uses a potato, and water with sugar dissolved in it, to show how osmosis works.

OSMOSIS IN ACTION

You will need:

✔ Two small plates
✔ A safe vegetable knife
✔ A teaspoon
✔ Water
✔ Table salt or sugar
✔ A large potato

1 Being careful with the knife, cut the potato in half, and peel a 0.5 inch (1 cm) strip around the edge of each half. Now cut a small, square hollow out of the peel side of each potato half.

2 Put a spoonful of sugar, or table salt, into the hollow on the side of one potato half. Take care not to spill any out of the hollow. If you do, brush it off with a dry cloth.

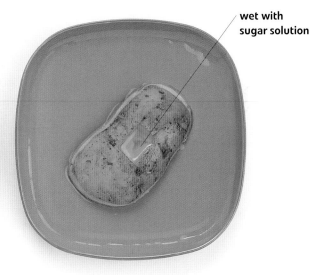

3 Lay each potato half on a dish with the flat, cut side down. Carefully pour water around the outside of each. The water should just come up to the top of the peeled strip. Leave to stand.

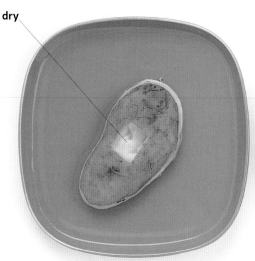

CLOSE-UP *Osmosis*

Osmosis occurs with solutions. Solutions are liquids (usually water) in which solid chemicals are dissolved. That means the solids are so broken up and mixed in they seem part of the liquid. When a lot of solid is dissolved in a solution, the solution is said to be strong or concentrated. Osmosis occurs when solutions of different strengths are on either side of a membrane dotted with pores (holes), called a semipermeable membrane. The pores must be just big enough to let small molecules of water ooze through. Yet they must not be so big they let through bigger molecules of solids dissolved in the water. When osmosis starts, water from the weaker or less concentrated solution oozes through the pores to mix with the stronger or more conctntrated solution. This slowly weakens the stronger solution. Water goes on oozing through from the weaker solution until both solutions are exactly the same strength.

dry

wet with sugar solution

Water transportation

Look at the potato halves after a day or so. You should find that the hollow of one is filled with water, while the other is dry. The one filled with water is the one you put sugar or salt in. The water has been drawn through the potato into the hollow by osmosis. In osmosis, water always moves from places where a solution is weak to places where it is strong. Here, the sugar or salt makes a strong solution, while the water in the dish is a weak solution. So the water is drawn from the dish to the sugar or salt.

Did you know?
Most plants die in seawater. The high concentration of salt in seawater prevents them from taking up water by osmosis.

Building blocks of life

The simplest forms of life, such as bacteria and many algae, exist as just a single cell. A few kinds of single-celled algae live together in colonies. Yet most plants and animals are multicellular organisms. That means they are made up of thousands, or even millions, of cells.

Multicellular organisms are different from colonies of single cells because they are made of many different kinds of cells. These cells are specialized, which means each kind has its own particular task. But they work together to keep the organism alive. It is this working together, or organization, that is the key feature of multicellular organisms.

While single cells have to do everything themselves, multicelled organisms divide the tasks among all the different cells. In this way, the organisms can grow very big and complicated. This also allows such multicelled organisms to be much more independent of their surroundings than single-celled creatures.

Made of muscle
Like this powerful tiger, animals are largely made of muscle tissue. Muscle tissue is made of long, thin cells. These cells can strongly contract, or pull themselves shorter. They can then relax (lengthen) again.

Cells working together

The simplest multicellular organisms are creatures like sponges and jellyfish. In some ways, sponges are like large colonies of single-celled organisms, since they are made mostly of identical cells clumped together. But they also have some specialized cells, and this is what makes them different. Jellyfish are more organized and have well-defined structures.

Most multicellular plants and animals are even more highly organized. The cells are grouped together to make tissues. Each tissue is made of similar cells packed together, each doing the same task.

An animal's brain, for example, is made from nerve tissue. Nerve tissue is made from nerve cells, or neurons. Neurons are very good at sending the electrical signals that carry messages around the brain. The animal's skin is made mostly of epithelial tissue. Epithelial tissue is made of three kinds of cell. Most mammals and birds are built from four main kinds of tissue: epithelial tissue, muscle tissue, nerve tissue, and connective tissue. (see Close-up: Connective tissue).

Organs

Within an animal's body, some tissues join in a highly organized way to form organs such as the heart, lungs, liver, and stomach. Each organ has its own specialized task. The heart pumps blood. The lungs take in air. The stomach digests food, and so on. Beyond this, some organs are grouped together to make organ systems, like the respiratory (breathing) system.

CLOSE-UP *Connective tissue*

Connective tissue fills the spaces between other tissues and holds them together. It comes in many forms, including fat, cartilage, and tendons. Cartilage is a rubbery substance that acts as a cushion between bones. Tendons are fibers that tie muscles to bone. Bone and blood are also connective tissues. Most connective tissue is made mainly of fibroblasts, cells that make fibers. It is also made of two other things: fibers made by the cells, and matrix. Fibers are tiny strings of protein (see page 31). Matrix is the material in which everything else is set, like eggs in an omelet. The matrix can be anything from a runny syrup to a thick gel.

Did you know?
The natural sponge used in the shower for washing is not the flesh of a sponge. It is its skeleton.

Materials of life

Living things contain a lot of water. Besides water, three kinds of material play a key role in life: carbohydrates, lipids, and proteins. Carbohydrates are energy-rich substances such as sugars and starch. Animals take them from food to fuel their cells. Plants make their own for energy and to build cell walls with. Lipids are substances like fats and oils. They store energy and insulate animals against cold. Proteins are life's building materials, and are used to build anything from hair to muscles. They also have other functions, including acting as enzymes (see Close-up: Enzymes). These two experiments show enzymes at work and how to detect starch in food.

LOOKING FOR ENZYMES AND STARCH

You will need:

✔ Two strips of cotton
✔ Laundry detergent with enzymes and without
✔ Jelly or egg yolk

✔ Crackers
✔ Iodine
✔ A teaspoon and cup
✔ Two dishes

ENZYMES AT WORK

1 Smear jelly or egg yolk on two cotton strips. Mix a spoonful of each detergent in separate dishes with equal amounts of water. Dip one smeared strip in each dish and leave to soak for 30 minutes.

2 As you pull the strips out, you should find that the strip dipped in the detergent with enzymes is cleaner. This is because jelly and egg contain proteins that are broken down by enzymes.

TESTING FOR STARCH

1 Mix a drop of iodine into a cup of water. Put a piece of cracker into each of two clean dishes. Now drop a teaspoon of the iodine water onto one of the crackers only.

Eating energy

Take the cracker with no iodine from the dish and suck it until it is soggy. Return it to the dish and drop a teaspoon of iodine water on it, just as with the other cracker.

CLOSE-UP *Enzymes*

Enzymes are very important helper substances. They speed up the chemical changes on which all life depends. Without them, the changes would happen very slowly or not at all. Each enzyme is a protein adapted to speed up a particular chemical process. They work by bringing particular chemicals together and making them react. The enzyme gets the chemical change going but does not change itself. So it can do the task again and again. Some enzymes help break complex substances into simpler ones. Enzymes in an animal's digestive system help change foods into the right liquids. These liquids can be absorbed into the blood, then transported around the body. Other enzymes help build complex materials from simple ones. Enzymes in cells help turn food into building materials.

By turning the cracker purple, iodine indicates the presence of the carbohydrate starch in the dry cracker.

Iodine does not turn the sucked cracker purple. This is because your saliva has begun to dissolve the starch.

Did you know?

A single enzyme molecule can sometimes do its job a million times a minute.

How living things grow

Did you know?
Nerve cells are among the few cells that grow only once and are never replaced.

In single-celled organisms, the life of the cell is the life span of the organism. Most plants and animals are made from many cells, however. The life of each individual cell in an organism is usually quite short, much shorter than the life span of the whole plant or animal.

Why new cells are made

Cells are short-lived for two reasons. First of all, most cells only work well for a limited time. So a plant or animal stays healthy and lives longer by constantly replacing them as they become worn out. This is often a very rapid process. Skin cells in the human body, for instance, live only a day. So billions of new ones must be made each day.

Secondly, and even more importantly, a short cell life helps the plant or animal grow. As living things grow, the cells within them stay much the same size. The organism grows by gaining extra cells. The new cells are made as cells split in half, or divide, again and again. This is also how cells are made to replace worn out cells.

CLOSE-UP *Cells for new life*

Most animals and plants have two sets of instruction units or chromosomes (see page 22) in each cell. One set is from each parent. The mixing of chromosomes allows offspring to inherit the characteristics of not just one but both parents. Before a new life can begin, sex cells with just one set of chromosomes are made. This is done by a type of cell division called meiosis. Then to make a new life, two sex cells must join, one from each parent. Each brings its one set of chromosomes. This is what happens when flowers are pollinated or animals mate. Each parent of the new plant or animal donates one sex cell and one set of chromosomes. The joining of these two cells is called fertilization, or conception, and is the start of a new life. The fertilized cell with combined chromosomes is called a zygote.

CLOSE-UP *Cell division*

Cells usually divide by a process called mitosis. Mitosis is how cells divide to make new cells for growing or for replacing worn out cells. Cells for making offspring divide in a different way (see Close-up: Cells for new life). Mitosis makes two cells identical to the original cell. So the first stage is always the copying, or replication, of the basic instructions or DNA in the cell's nucleus. The DNA then coils up into X-shaped bundles called chromosomes. Each is made of two identical threads, or chromatids. As the cell starts to divide, the nucleus dissolves, and the chromatids are drawn to opposite sides of the cell. The cell stretches out like a sausage, and the chromatids bunch at each end. The middle of the cell narrows until it eventually splits to form two new cells.

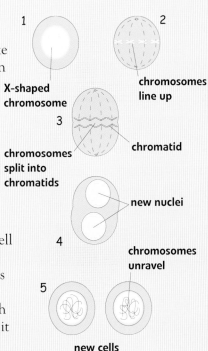

X-shaped chromosome

chromosomes line up

chromosomes split into chromatids

chromatid

new nuclei

chromosomes unravel

new cells

1. First, the DNA copies itself and coils up into X-shaped chromosomes.

2. The nucleus of the cell dissolves and chromosomes line up across the middle of the cell.

3. The chromatids of each pair are then drawn apart.

4. The chromatids move to each end of the cell and a new nucleus forms around the cluster of chromatids at each end.

5. The cell finally splits in two between the nuclei, leaving two new cells identical to the original cell. The chromosomes unravel.

Calf to cow
A calf will grow into a cow like its mother as the cells in its body divide and multiply over and over again.

Sharing instructions

When a cell divides, each new cell must have all the right components. The organelles are easily divided between the two halves. But a cell has only one set of chromosomes, which are threads of DNA that carry all the cell's instructions (see Passing life on, pages 22–23). So each time a cell splits, it first makes a copy of all its DNA. This way each of the new cells has its own copy.

Did you know?
The fastest dividing cells of all are often cancer cells, which divide uncontrollably.

Miracle of life

All living things reproduce: that is, produce offspring. Many animals and plants reproduce sexually. In animals, a sperm (male sex cell) fertilizes (combines with) an egg (female sex cell). Young animals hatch or develop from fertilized eggs. In plants, pollen with sperm from the male part of a flower fertilizes an ovule (egg) from the female part. The ovule then develops into a seed from which new plants will grow. Some organisms reproduce without sex. Amoebas simply split in two. Hydra (see On the track: Pond life, page 7) and sea anemones grow a bud on the side of their bodies that develops into a new animal and breaks off. The experiment here shows how you can see the miracle of life in action as tiny brine shrimps hatch from their eggs.

HATCHING BRINE SHRIMPS

You will need:

- ✔ A glass bowl
- ✔ Liquid fish food from an aquarium store
- ✔ Brine shrimp eggs from an aquarium store
- ✔ A magnifying glass
- ✔ Water
- ✔ A spoon
- ✔ Sea salt

CLOSE-UP *Embryos*

Once an egg is fertilized by a sperm cell, the egg cell splits in two. These two cells split into four, the four into eight, and so on (see Close-up: Cell division, page 19). Once a fertilized egg divides like this it is known as an embryo. This is a growing ball of cells that will become the new animal or plant. In birds, fishes, reptiles, and amphibians such as frogs, the embryo is contained inside a shelled egg. The embryo grows using food stored in the yolk. In most mammals, the embryo grows in a pocket in the mother's body called the uterus. It is supplied with food from her blood through a spongy surface called the placenta. In humans, the embryo is called a fetus after two months. Once the embryo has developed into a new animal, an egg will hatch or a baby will be born.

1 Fill a bowl with tepid water. Stir in about three tablespoonfuls of sea salt until it dissolves. When the water is completely cold, add a few drops of liquid fish food.

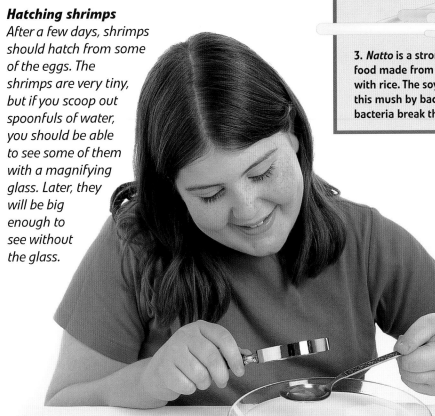

2 Sprinkle a teaspoonful of brine shrimp eggs into the water. Leave the bowl in a warm place, such as on a radiator, so that the temperature stays around or above 70 °F (21 °C).

Hatching shrimps

After a few days, shrimps should hatch from some of the eggs. The shrimps are very tiny, but if you scoop out spoonfuls of water, you should be able to see some of them with a magnifying glass. Later, they will be big enough to see without the glass.

ON THE TRACK *Life in food*

Tiny forms of life thrive almost everywhere. Food provides a rich habitat for microorganisms. Although they are far too small to see except under a microscope, you can tell they are there from their effect on the food.

1. Yeast is a microscopic fungus. It breaks sugars down to make the alcohol in beer and the gas that makes bread rise. This is called fermentation.

1

2. Without a bacteria called lactobacillus, yogurt would just be old milk. The bacteria feast on the sugars in milk and convert it to yogurt. In the process, they make an acid that turns the yogurt sour. This helps keep other microorganisms away.

2

3

3. *Natto* is a strong-smelling, mushy Japanese food made from soybeans that is usually served with rice. The soybeans are transformed into this mush by bacteria called *Bacilis subtilis*. The bacteria break the beans down by fermentation.

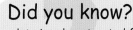

Did you know?
Chocolate is only extracted from the pods it grows on with the help of lactobacilli and acetobacter bacteria.

Passing life on

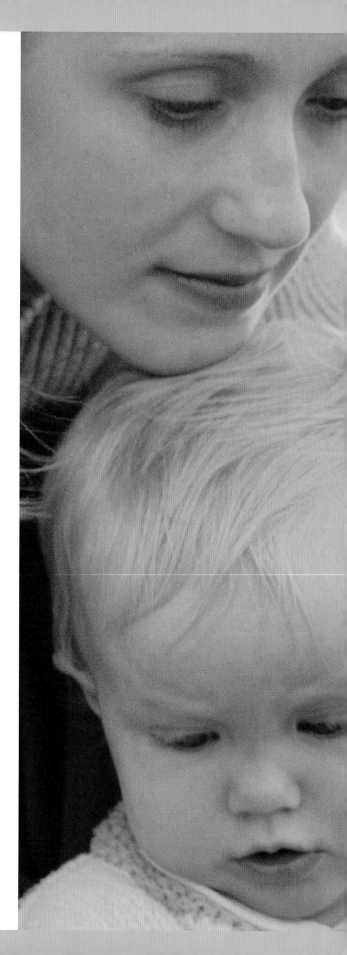

Many children look a lot like their parents. In fact, every plant and animal closely resembles not only its parents but even its grandparents. This family resemblance is called heredity. It depends on genes, the life instructions carried as a chemical code inside the nucleus of every living cell.

Genes carry the plans for building cells, tissues, organs, and even complete bodies. They provide instructions for making chemicals called proteins. Proteins are the basic building blocks of the body. Some features of an animal's body are determined by a single gene. Most depend on a group.

Genes not only pass on family traits, but also allow tiny differences called variations. So no two plants or animals are exactly alike. This is vital since variations allow species to change and develop (see Life moves on, pages 24–25).

Chromosomes

Genes are carried by the chemical molecule DNA (see Close-up: DNA and genes). In a living cell, each molecule of DNA forms a thread called a chromosome. Chromosomes can be thought of as the cell's instruction books. Genes are the sentences in this book.

Every plant or animal has a particular number of chromosomes in its cells. Human body cells have 46 chromosomes. Of these,

CLOSE-UP *DNA and genes*

DNA molecules can only be seen under powerful microscopes. Yet they are big compared to other molecules. They are thin, but very long. Each molecule is made from two strands wrapped around each other like a twisted rope ladder. The key to DNA's power lies in the "rungs" of the ladder. Each rung is made of a pair of bases. The order, or sequence, of base pairs is a code that provides life's instructions. Sequences of pairs work a bit like words that tell the cell what to do. These words, in turn, build up into sentences of instructions called genes. Each tells the cell to make a certain protein. Humans have about 40,000 genes; fruit flies have 13,000. The total is called the genome.

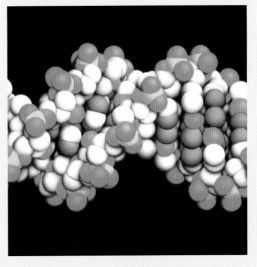

A short section of a model of the long, twisted DNA molecule.

22 always come in matching pairs. The final pair is different in men and women. These sex chromosomes control whether a baby is a boy or a girl. Girls have matching X-shaped sex chromosomes. Boys have one X-shaped chromosome and one Y-shaped one.

Apart from the sex chromosomes, all chromosomes come in matching pairs. So there are two genes for every body feature. One is from the mother, and one from the father. Paired genes are called alleles. Some alleles are dominant; others are recessive. A dominant allele, like that for brown eyes, is always expressed. That is, it always shows in the body. A recessive allele, like that for blue eyes, is shut out by a dominant allele. Blue eyes only occur when two blue alleles meet.

Did you know?

DNA is short for deoxyribonucleic acid. It is made mainly of carbon, hydrogen, and oxygen.

Life moves on

Today, there is an astonishing variety of life on Earth. Yet every plant and animal has its own natural home or way of living. Some plants thrive in deserts, for example, while others prefer cold, damp places. Similarly, some animals eat only meat, while others eat grass. Every living thing, it seems, is very well suited, or adapted, to its lifestyle.

In 1859, an English scientist named Charles Darwin explained this with his theory of evolution. He suggested that over millions of years, plant and animal species gradually change, or evolve, as they adapt to their surroundings.

How evolution works

The idea of evolution depends on the fact that no two living things are exactly alike. This means some individual plants or animals may start life with features that help them survive better than their fellows. One animal, for instance, might have long legs that help it escape predators. Or a plant might have big leaves that help it grow better in shady places. Animals and plants that have these helpful features are likely to live longer. And if they live longer, they are

Hand-me-downs
An orangutan's hands and feet are ideal for swinging through branches and gripping food. They developed gradually through millions of years of evolution.

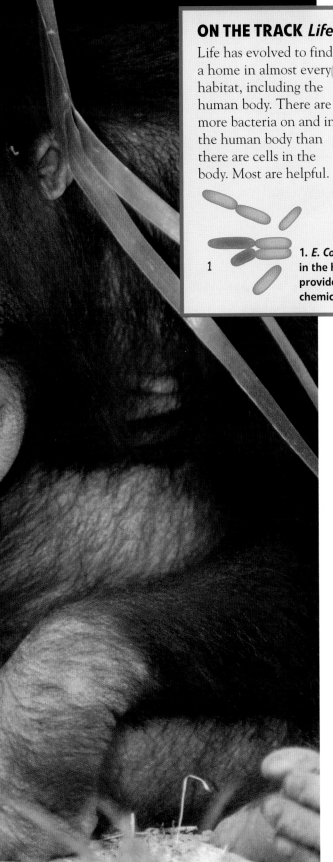

ON THE TRACK *Life in the body*

Life has evolved to find a home in almost every habitat, including the human body. There are more bacteria on and in the human body than there are cells in the body. Most are helpful.

3. Helicobacter are bacteria that live in the stomach. They normally help digestion. But if they grow too numerous, they can cause stomach ulcers.

2. Methanobacteria live in the intestine. They break down carbohydrates. But as they do, they make the gas that comes out as wind.

4. Streptococcus are bacteria that live in the mouth. They help break down sugary food. But if they are fed too much sugar, the acid they make causes tooth cavities.

1. *E. Coli* are bacteria that live in the human intestine. They provide the body with useful chemicals like Vitamins K and B.

more likely to have offspring that inherit these features. Those without the useful features are less likely to survive. This is called natural selection. Slowly, over many generations, better adapted animals and plants survive and thrive. Others die out or find a new home or way of life. In this way, Darwin believed, every different species of plant and animal slowly evolved.

Fossils are the remains, or traces, of long-dead plants and animals, preserved by being turned to stone. By looking at fossils dating from different periods of the past, experts have found that things happened as Darwin suggested. But not all experts think change comes so slowly and steadily. Some believe changes come in rapid bursts, with long periods in between when few things change.

Did you know?

In theory, all animals, including humans, evolved from sea creatures that lived 500 million years ago.

Game of life

During their lifetime, most animals produce many offspring. If every one of them grew up to have young of their own, the world would soon become overcrowded. In fact, only a few usually survive. Humans are unusual, for most of their offspring do survive. Other creatures are more like octopuses. Only one or two of an octopus's 200,000 offspring live long enough to have their own babies. Offspring that do survive are often the ones best suited to the conditions, and best able to find the food they need. These "fit" individuals survive to pass their features on to their offspring. Within a few generations, there are more of these fit animals and fewer unfit ones. So each kind of animal changes or evolves by this process of natural selection. This game shows how it works.

Select colors
The striking colors of this butterfly have developed through countless generations of natural selection.

Did you know?
When some people talk about natural selection, they sum it up as "survival of the fittest."

**CARD GAME:
HOW STRONG
GENES SELECT
THEMSELVES**

You will need:

✔ A group of at least four card players

✔ A deck of cards

1 Deal out seven cards to each player. Imagine the cards are the genes for life. Diamonds are the trump suit, the suit that beats all other suits. So diamonds represent strong genes that give a player a better chance of survival.

CLOSE-UP *Mutations*

Natural selection is thought to work through changes that happen entirely by chance. A creature's genetic instructions are contained in DNA molecules (see Close-up: DNA and genes, page 23). These make sure an organism looks very much like its parents and that it has the same characteristics. But there are always slight mistakes, or mutations, in the DNA. These mutations occur when the DNA is being copied to make the sex cells from which the offspring will develop. This is why no two animals look exactly alike. Sometimes, mutations can be more dramatic. Often an offspring with such dramatic mutations dies soon after it is born. Sometimes, however, the mutation can give the offspring an extra edge in the battle for survival. The offspring may have longer legs for escaping from predators, for example, or slightly sharper eyes for catching prey.

2 Each player in turn lays down one card of the same suit (heart, club, etc.), until all have laid a card. If a player has no card of the same suit, they play a diamond—a strong gene. After playing a diamond, pick it up and save it for the next round. If a player has no diamond either, play any card.

3 The player who plays the highest card or highest diamond wins the round, and begins the next. Once all seven cards have been played, the player who has won the fewest rounds drops out. The winner starts a new game by dealing six cards to each survivor. Each player then picks up their diamonds from the previous round and discards one card for each diamond they pick up.

Count down
Now play out all six cards in rounds as before. Again, the player who has won the fewest rounds at the end of the game must drop out. Continue by playing new games as shown in steps 2 and 3, first with five cards each, then with four cards, then with three, and so on. If you get down to two players, the loser should not drop out until they fail to win a single round. The last player surviving has survived by natural selection. There is a high chance this was because they gained extra diamonds, or strong genes, as the game went on.

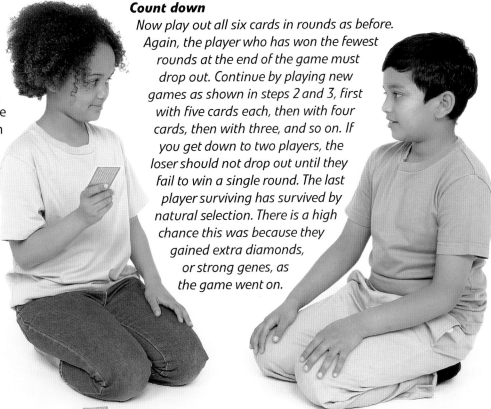

Identifying living things

Scientists know of more than 1.5 million kinds of animals, 350,000 kinds of plants, and many hundreds of thousands of kinds of microorganisms. Earth may be home to several million more creatures. Identifying and grouping all these living things is a huge task. Scientists start by placing each living thing in one of five giant groups, or kingdoms: animals, plants, fungi, protists, and bacteria (or prokaryotes).

ANIMAL KINGDOM

 VERTEBRATES: Animals with backbones, including mammals, fish, reptiles, and birds.

 INVERTEBRATES: Animals without backbones, including insects, spiders, and shellfish.

PLANT KINGDOM

 ANGIOSPERMS: Plants with flowers, including wildflowers, grasses, cereals, and many trees.

 GYMNOSPERMS: Plants with cones, including conifers such as pines, ginkgos, and cycads.

 VASCULAR PLANTS: Plants that reproduce with spores, including ferns and mosses.

FUNGI KINGDOM

 Includes yeast, mushrooms, toadstools, mildews, and molds.

PROTIST KINGDOM

 Plant and animal-like microorganisms, including amoebas and algae. Also, seaweeds.

BACTERIA KINGDOM (PROKARYOTES)*

 Divided into EUBACTERIA and ARCHAEBACTERIA, which are the most ancient.

*Some scientists group eubacteria and archaebacteria into two separate kingdoms.

VERTEBRATES
Nearly all the larger animals are vertebrates, which are animals with backbones.

Distinguishing feature:
• Beside a backbone, most vertebrates' bodies have a framework or skeleton of bone.

Mammals: Class MAMMALIA
There are about 4,000 known kinds of mammals. They are warm-blooded, and most are covered in fur. This allows mammals to live in cold parts of the world. Mammals feed their young on milk from the mother's teats. Most young are born as babies.
Mammals include: *Dogs, cats, horses, mice, cattle*

Birds: Class AVES
There are about 9,000 known kinds of birds. Like mammals they are warm-blooded, but they are covered in feathers, not fur. Birds have two wings. Female birds lay their young as eggs.
Birds include: *Sparrows, thrushes, eagles, ducks*

Amphibians: Class AMPHIBIA
There are about 4,200 known kinds of amphibians. They are cold-blooded and hatch from eggs as tadpoles. They generally begin their lives in water, then spend much of their adult lives on land.
Amphibians include: *Frogs, toads, newts, caecilians*

Reptiles: Class REPTILIA
There about 6,300 known kinds of reptiles. All are cold-blooded, and most hatch from eggs. The young look like small adults. Unlike amphibians, most spend much of their lives on land.
Reptiles include: *Turtles, tuataras, snakes, alligators*

Fish: Classes include OSTEICHTHYES (Bony fish)
There are about 25,000 kinds of fish. Most live in water, breathe through gills, and hatch from eggs. Most are bony fish, which have skeletons of bone like other vertebrates. Other fish, including sharks, rays, and lampreys, have rubbery cartilage instead.
Fish include: *Cod, trout, salmon, goldfish, sharks*

INVERTEBRATES

Most of the smaller animals are invertebrates. There are more than 1 million kinds.

Distinguishing feature:
• Invertebrates have no bones, but many have a hard shell or casing called an exoskeleton.

Arthropods: Phylum ARTHROPODA
The 800,000 or so arthropods include insects, spiders, and crustaceans such as crabs. As adults, insects have six legs and usually wings, too. They go through dramatic changes in their life cycle. Spiders have eight legs, and crabs have ten.
Arthropods include: *Flies, butterflies, bees, lobsters*

Sponges: Phylum PORIFERA
There are about 10,000 kinds of sponges. All live in water, mostly in the sea. Bath sponges are made from the skeletons of living sponges. Sponges cannot see, hear, or even move.
Sponges include: *Loggerhead sponges, leaf sponges*

Mollusks: Phylum MOLLUSCA
There are 45,000 kinds of mollusks, including squids and octopuses, the biggest of invertebrates. All have soft bodies but many, like snails and shellfish such as clams, have a tough shell.
Mollusks include: *Snails, slugs, limpets, octopuses*

Cnidarians: Phylum CNIDARIA
There are 8,500 kinds of cnidarians. They are sea creatures with a soft tube for a body and no head, tail, or limbs. There are stinging tentacles around the tube mouth. In jellyfish, the tube is flattened to a bell shape. Many attach themselves to rocks.
Cnidarians include: *Jellyfish, sea anemones, corals*

Worms: Phylum ANNELIDA, NEMATODA, PLATYHELMINTHES
There are 45,000 kinds of worms. All have long, thin, soft bodies. There are three groups: "segmented" worms with marked body sections, pipe-shaped "round" worms, and tape-shaped "flat" worms.
Worms include: *Tapeworms, flukes, bristleworms*

ANGIOSPERMS

About 90 percent of all plants are angiosperms, or flowering plants.

Distinguishing feature:
• Grow from seeds made by flowers.

Monocotyledons: Class LILIOPSIDAE
About 70,000 kinds of flowering plants are monocotyledons, or monocots. When they first grow from seed, monocots have just a single seed leaf, or cotyledon. Most have soft green stems.
Monocots include: *Lilies, tulips, bluebells, orchids*

Dicotyledons: Class MAGNOLIOPSIDAE
About 150,000 kinds of flowering plants are dicotyledons, or dicots. When dicots first grow from seed, they have two seed leaves, or cotyledons. They include trees with woody stems.
Dicots include: *Magnolias, oaks, peonies, roses*

GYMNOSPERMS

Most other large plants, apart from angiosperms, are gymnosperms.

Distinguishing feature:
• Grow from seeds, mostly made in cones.

Conifers: Class CONIFEROPHYTA
There are about 500 kinds of conifers. Most are tall, dark green forest trees. They are mostly evergreen, with needlelike leaves that stay on the tree throughout the winter.
Conifers include: *Firs, pines, redwoods, larches*

Cycads, ginkgos: Class CYCADOPHYTA, GINKGOPHYTA
Cycads and ginkgos are mostly trees. Cycads look a little like palm trees. They were once widespread, but have become rare since the emergence of angiosperms 100 million years ago.
The only surviving ginkgo is the *maidenhair tree.*

VASCULAR PLANTS

Vascular plants, like mosses and ferns, grow from long-lasting cells called spores.

Distinguishing feature:
• Tiny spore capsules on leaves or stalks.

Mosses: Division Bryophyta
Mosses and liverworts grow on walls, rocks, and old logs. They have no true roots. They take moisture from the air through their stems and tiny rootlike threads called rhizoids.

Bryophytes inlcude: *Sphagnum moss, hornwort*

Club mosses, ferns: Division Lycophyta, Pteridophyta
Club mosses, ferns, and horsetails are called featherplants because they have feathery leaves called fronds. Unlike mosses, they also have roots.

Ferns include: *Bracken, giant polypody, maidenhair fern, climbing fern, ladder brake*

PROTISTS

Most protists are single-celled organisms, and nearly all of microscopic size.

Distinguishing feature:
• Plantlike and animal-like organisms.

Protozoa: Division Protozoa
Protozoa are single-celled organisms that vary from very simple amoebas to ciliates, which have tiny hairs that help them move about.

Protozoa include: *Amoeba, euglena, trypanosomes*

Algae: Division Algae
Algae are simple organisms that live in water and moist soil. Most are microscopic and consist of one cell. But there are exceptions, such as seaweeds. Like plants, algae have chlorophyll, which helps them make food from sunlight by photosynthesis.

Algaes include: *Diatoms, seaweed (brown algae)*

FUNGI

Fungi often grow in the ground like plants and feed on living or rotting matter.

Distinguishing feature:
• Most feed through threads called hyphae.

Mushrooms and toadstools: Class Basidiomycetes
Many fungi spread their hyphae through soil or wood. Mushrooms and toadstools are the parts of these fungi that appear in a clump on the surface.

Mushrooms and toadstools include: *Field mushrooms, fly agarics, puffballs, bracket fungi, destroying angels, death caps*

Molds and mildews: Division Mycota
Molds and mildews are the furry growths often seen on rotting bread and fruit. The fur is a mass of tiny hyphae. Many provide bacteria-killing drugs.

Molds include: *Aspergillus, penicillium*

BACTERIA

Bacteria are microscopic organisms that are made of a single cell.

Distinguishing feature:
• The cell has no nucleus (control center).

Bacteria: Subkingdom Eubacteria
The eubacteria are the simplest of all living things. They come in three basic shapes: balls, rods, and spirals. Like plants, cyanobacteria (once known as blue-green algae) can make food using sunlight.

Bacteria include: *E. coli, streptococcus, lactobacillus*

Archaebacteria: Subkingdom Archaea
The Archaea are the oldest forms of life on Earth. They are similar to bacteria but live in extreme places—either very salty or very, very hot.

Archaea include: *Halobacterium*

Glossary

archaea The most ancient form of life, a micro-organism that can live in very hot or salty places.

bacterium (plural **bacteria**) Single-celled microscopic organism with no cell nucleus.

carbohydrate Organic substances such as sugar and starch that animals eat for energy.

cell Basic unit of life—a microscopic package of liquids surrounded by a membrane or skin.

chromosome X-shaped packages of doubled-up DNA. They are split during meiosis and mitosis, sharing the DNA between new cells.

cyanobacteria Bacteria that can use the sun's energy to make their own food, as plants do.

chlorophyll The green or purple substance in plants that captures the sun's energy.

cytoplasm The mixture of chemicals and structures inside a living cell outside the nucleus.

DNA Deoxyribonucleic acid, the chemical strands inside every living cell that carry all life's instructions as a chemical code.

embryo Earliest stage in the development of a living thing.

eukaryote Living thing whose cells have a nucleus—that is, all but bacteria.

evolution The development of new species over long periods of time.

gene A segment of DNA that carries the code for a particular physical characteristic.

meiosis The way cells divide to create the sex cells (sperm and egg) needed to start a new life.

membrane A cell's thin skin.

mitosis The way cells divide into identical cells for normal growth or replacing worn out cells.

mutation Chance change in a gene or a whole chromosome that gives offspring a new feature.

nucleus The central package in certain kinds of living cell that contains the cell's DNA.

organ Body part with particular function, such as the heart or liver.

organelle Small object inside a living cell.

organism A living thing such as a plant, protist, animal, fungi, or bacterium.

osmosis Slow oozing between plant cells of liquids containing dissolved chemicals.

ovule Egg that will turn into an embryo.

photosynthesis The way leaves use the sun's energy to make sugar from air and water.

prokaryote Living thing whose cells have no nucleus—that is, bacteria, including archaea.

protein The basic building material of all living things.

starch Energy food made by plants.

tissue Body material made by groups of cells.

virus Very tiny particle that can reproduce itself inside the cells of living things.

FURTHER READING:
David Burnie. *Life.* New York: Dorling Kindersley, 1994.

Bobbie Kalman. *What is a Living Thing?* New York: Crabtree, 1999.

Bobbie Kalman, Jacqueline Langille. *What is a Life Cycle?* New York: Crabtree, 1998.

Kenneth G. Rainis and Bruce J. Russell. *Guide to Microlife.* New York: Orchard Books, 1998.Corinne Stockley, Kirsten Rogers, Carrie A Seay. *Ilustrated Dictionary of Biology.* Duluth, GA: Usborne, 2001.

Index